I am a peak in God, and upward must I pace
Upon myself, that God may show His tender face.

—Angelus Silesius

# Release for Trapped Christians

FLORA SLOSSON WUELLNER

Nashville　　　Abingdon Press　　　New York

*Library of Congress Cataloging in Publication Data*

WUELLNER, FLORA SLOSSON. Release for trapped Christians.
1. Prayer. 2. Spiritual life. I. Title.
BV210.2.W815      248'.4      73-20034
*ISBN 0-687-35936-8*

Scripture quotations are from the Revised Standard Version of
the Bible, copyrighted 1946, 1952, 1971 by the Division of
Christian Education, National Council of Churches, and are
used by permission.

The lines by Angelus Silesius are translated by Carol North
Valhope and are from *The Soul Afire: Revelations of the
Mystics,* edited by H. A. Reinhold, copyright © Pantheon
Books, a Division of Random House, Inc.

MANUFACTURED BY THE PARTHENON PRESS AT
NASHVILLE, TENNESSEE, UNITED STATES OF AMERICA

Dedicated to my husband, Wilhelm,
Companion in this way of Release

# Contents

# 1-The Trap

This is a handbook of release for those of us who are trying to grow spiritually but have found ourselves trapped along the way.

How the religious scene has changed in the last five years! It is an exciting time to be alive and spiritually alert and growing.

As we entered the 1970s, *Life* magazine reported, "Never before in history has a single society taken up such a wide range of religious and near-religious systems at once." And the religious resurgence continues to grow. Whereas just a few years ago the individual searcher was left pretty much alone and unguided in his spiritual exploration, now it is a problem which of the many groups, guides, or paths to choose.

We have not only the explosively radiant charismatic Christian groups, the rapidly growing meditation groups with their mystical insights from the Far East, the tremendous range of occult and psychic development groups, but also the new spiritual concern in our ordinary churches. An extraordinary number of middle-class, middle-of-the-road churches have experienced a profound swing around to depth concerns:

prayer retreats, communion groups, healing services, meditation training.

The genuine power of prayer is no longer surprising news. Many of us have seen with our own eyes the sick healed, the despairing raised to new life, the aimless burning with new enthusiasm. We have seen with our own eyes drug addicts, alcoholics, and compulsive eaters and smokers lifted out of their traps.

Many of us ordinary Christians have learned firsthand that Jesus' comparison of God's power to light, fire, growing plants was not exaggerated. These days we are using also such examples as atomic energy, X rays, cobalt, and electric power to try to describe what God's power can do.

Where in all this fresh, exciting enthusiasm can there be a serious problem, a widespread problem in our growing?

It is simply this. I have seen increasingly how after the first, joyous experience of healing, conversion, prayer power, or the discovery of a new and helpful spiritual way, sooner or later there seems to spread a blight of fatigue, tension, a mechanical going through the motions, or rigid compulsiveness, in the place of radiant freedom.

I noticed it first in myself after the first few years of joyful enthusiasm. Why did I begin to dread the ringing of the telephone? Why did I so often feel tired and drained after a prayer meeting or a counseling?

I noticed it in a friend, a strong spiritual leader increasingly tormented by strong emotions, oversensitivity, bad dreams.

What was the problem with the woman who had so

radiantly hailed the new life, who had so generously given herself to church work, and now was seriously ill with high blood pressure?

Why, I wondered, were so many ministers and theological leaders (and prayer group members) going to psychiatrists?

And what had happened to a certain little group, once so loving, so on fire with the Spirit, which had degenerated into a rigid, fault-finding, ingrown cell, insisting that all members read their letters aloud, allowing no member to make any private decisions?

Is it that we had all seriously sinned, and God had taken his Holy Spirit from us? Or had our expectations of God and prayer been too high? Should we have tried harder, and forced our enthusiasm higher? Were we just plain selfish and egocentric? Should we try a harder discipline? Was God testing us with a "dark night of the soul"?

It took me a long time to learn that it was none of those things. We had not seriously sinned. We were not monsters of selfishness. Neither God nor the power of prayer had abandoned us, nor were we being tested.

*We had fallen into a trap,* in spite of all our good intentions and our efforts.

Oddly enough, just as I began writing this page, I heard a wild fluttering of wings on the other side of a little stone wall in our garden. I investigated and found a young robin who had flown into the center of a large coil of chicken wire. He was dashing himself against the mesh, bewildered and frustrated. He still had his wings. The free air was around him, and the blue sky and leafy branches above him. He had the power to fly. But what had happened? Why could he only flutter and hop instead of soaring?

After releasing him, I went back to my seat and took a long look at myself. That bird was me. That bird was many of my fellow pilgrims. We had given ourselves to Christ. We had been released magnificently from so many old habits and compulsions. Prayer was like wings, and we had known, for a while, what it was to fly with power.

But somehow, we had flown into a trap. The name of the trap is "imitation." *The trap is not that we became bad, but that we began to imitate the good.*

The trap is that, without being aware of it, we have made a *Christian image* for ourselves, in place of surrender to the living Christ himself.

We chose a blueprint, a set of rules about how we should act and feel, rather than a living, changing adventure.

There are definite signs of this entrapment. It takes both courage and honesty to face them. It is hard to admit that we have fallen out of life and out of freedom.

Let us ask ourselves these questions:

Do I feel chronic guilt about my life as a Christian? Do I feel I am never really pleasing God enough, or living up to the expectations of others? Do others seem more like "real" Christians than I do?

Do I often feel tired or depressed when serving others, or when praying?

Do I use the words "ought" and "should" a great

deal about myself and others—"I shouldn't feel that way," or, "Christians ought to . . ." etc.?

Do I often find myself doing things I don't really want to do, because I feel it is my "Christian duty"? Is it almost impossible to say no to any requested service? Do I feel nobody else will do it if I don't?

Am I usually ashamed of feelings of anger, loneliness, fear, doubt, desire, pride? Is it hard to share them with others? Am I afraid these feelings are unchristian or will block God's work through me?

Do I find myself forcing "positive" feelings of cheerfulness, optimism, love, courage, and trust?

Do I get very impatient with myself because I do not grow faster in the fruits and powers of the Spirit?

Do I increasingly feel that everything depends on me—*my* power of prayers, *my* love for others, *my* hard work? If a plan or relationship fails, do I always feel it is because I have not loved or worked or prayed hard enough?

Do I find it hard to let others be what they want to be, and to feel what they really feel? Is it hard to listen to them without advising, condemning, moralizing, pushing, either outwardly or inwardly?

If we find (as I did) that these things are true of us, it is a sign that we have drifted away from life *in* Christ into a forced, strained imitation of him.

We have substituted compulsive perfectionism for the unfolding mystery of the Spirit in us.

We have substituted command and obedience, duty and guilt, for the loving relationship of bride and bridegroom.

We have flown out of one box into another, and are

all the more bewildered because we did have a brief glimpse of what God's freedom is like.

We pray, but prayer seems to tighten the trap around us, to make it worse, because we are not really praying to the living God at all, but to some image we have set up in his place. Prayer is not an *automatic* release. It depends on *how* we are praying, and *to whom*.

In the name of "religion" we have entered into a state of mind which says:

> "Because I belong to Christ . . .
>    I ought to be a certain kind of person.
> I am *not* that kind of person
>    Therefore . . .
> I must *make* myself that person
>    By praying harder
>       working harder
>          loving harder . . .
> No matter how I really feel."

This is the trap.

# 2-The Shattered Image

Here is an experiment for you to try. Close your eyes and make a mental image of what you consider to be the perfect Christian man or woman. What is the expression on his face? What is he saying? What is he usually doing? How is he dressed? It doesn't matter that your image is probably not the same as mine. The point is that we each do have an image of the ideal Christian that is as clear and distinct as the image of the ideal housewife or the ideal businessman pictured in TV advertisements. We talk a lot about the "feminine mystique" or the "businessman's syndrome." Just as devastating is the "Christian mystique" or the "prayer mystique." It is all the more destructive because we each have our own particular one which has a stranglehold on our living spirit.

My image was always that of a quiet, grave lady. She is appropriately and quietly dressed. She is never untidy. She is busier in good works than anybody else, but never seems hurried or flurried! She is calmly efficient and infinitely loving as she takes on everyone else's burdens! She is never tired. She is never cross. She never needs anything for herself. Her voice

—never raised in annoyance—rings clear as a bell with authority and wisdom! She has every one of the gifts of the Spirit. She never feels fear or doubt or loneliness or personal longings. Other people feel them —but she is strong and calm enough to set them right! Everyone turns to her when something needs to be done—and she does it! She is God's perfect channel!

This lady has haunted me pretty persistently for many years. Anything about me which didn't fit into her image was obviously wrong and sinful. The discovery of the power of prayer about twelve years ago freed and released me from many things—but not from this lady! In fact, it entrenched her more deeply. *Now at last,* I felt, with prayer to help me, this lady would become a reality. Sometimes I would pretend I was her, so skillfully and unconsciously that only my best friends would spot the mask. Sometimes she would only make me feel acutely guilty when I was rushing around the kitchen at the end of a long day, hot and flustered. She rose and stared reproachfully if I got angry or felt tired. She made me feel inadequate and almost hopeless. I was so far from being her that obviously it would take years of stern prayer discipline to become her. Perhaps, I thought, it meant that I hadn't really found Christ in the first place! A kind of smog began to settle over the freshness of my Christian joy. Prayer often seemed to make it worse, not better. The promised energy would flow in—and then to come up against a block.

But if I rebelled against that "perfect" lady, I would remind myself that we Christians are supposed to grow and change. What better model could I grow toward?

*I had not yet learned that one thing almost as deadly as an Antichrist is a man-made imitation of Christ!* Why? Because with an imitation one deceives himself into believing that he has the living reality. You think you are free—but you are not.

I was not free from this lady of my own making until God showed me a parable in my garden. In our backyard we have two fruit trees—a flourishing apple tree and a healthy lemon bush. Each produces its own fruit in due season. Each gets energy and life from the soil, the rain, the sun. But what if one day the lemon bush looked at the apple tree and thought, *"There* is the ideal fruit tree! I am a fruit tree, and *that* is what I ought to be."* And then what if the lemon bush were to take the energy of the sun and soil—and use it to try to produce apples instead of lemons!

I see this happening in many lives: prayer-filled lives. I see so many of us taking in the energy of God through prayer, knowing that prayer produces miracles of change and growth—and then using this energy to bring about what *we* decide shall be the type and timing of our growth.

Growth? Yes. After some fixed model? No! Nothing was wrong in itself with my inner picture of that strong, ever-active lady. What was wrong was that I tried to force myself into her image. *We are not to imitate anybody—however noble.* The true freedom of Christ releases the deep, unique beauty which is in every one of us. God has created every one of us as a different facet of the great diamond reflecting glory.

Each of us has his own special reason for being in the world. Each of us has brought with him his own special gifts. Each of us will sing his own unique song of joy. What else is a universe like ours for, with its millions of evolving bodies and souls, except for the glory of its diversity in response to the one Light? If God wanted only one kind of response to his love, he would have made only one kind of form to look back at him. *We are not even to imitate Jesus. We are to abide in Jesus!*

The tragic truth is that the very gifts and powers our deep souls have tried to bring into this world are the very powers that we most sternly repress in ourselves—often in the name of religion. And the more our interest in religion grows, the more does this danger grow.

The release of the genuine, deep, unique self—that is what the living Christ can do for us. He tries to get through to us, to help us open the door to the light within, but we are so busy with our "oughts" and "shoulds" that we don't hear him.

I am increasingly suspicious of any religious movement or religious leader that tries to map out or blueprint our lives for us, or make our deep choices for us. I see a devastating spiritual dictatorship growing in many of our religious movements today, which is holding many spirits in thrall. Beware of any church, or any leader, or any teaching, which tries to tell you what you "ought" to do with your life, or what your own deep spirit looks like!

Beware of those parts in your own self that repress, shout down, ignore other parts of yourself!

18

Beware of any method of prayer or spiritual discipline which makes you feel more strained, anxious, burdened, guilty! For as the interest in and practice of prayer grow, so do the false, sick kinds of prayer built on fear of God and fear of the genuine release.

Prayer does not *automatically* release us. It can make us worse if it merely feeds life and energy into a false stereotype. It can make us worse if we are using it as an escape from facing the true self with its powers and problems.

But there *is* a prayer which can release us. Honest prayer. Prayer which increasingly delivers the depths of our bodies, minds, and spirits into the hands of God, trusting him to bring forth what is hidden there.

What *is* this kind of prayer? Lets look first at what it *isn't*.

Prayer is not one more burden and obligation added to all the other burdens and obligations of life.

Prayer is not an inscrutable God hiding while we seek.

Prayer is not some difficult, esoteric exercise based on willpower.

Prayer is not primarily a matter of emotions or mystical feelings (though they may be present).

Prayer is not explaining anything to God. He already knows about it.

Prayer is not pleading with God. He already wishes to give far more than we are willing to receive.

Prayer is not just for certain types of people or for certain moods. We can begin just where we are and as we are.

Prayer—above all—does not turn us into some

standardized type of person, some categorical image. It does not put us into any box—even a holy box.

What is the prayer that releases? Picture yourself in a small, confining dark hut. The windows and doors are bolted shut. You sit there, with perhaps a candle and matches to give you a feeble hint of light. One day you rise and go to the window, and slowly learn to open it. Perhaps the bolts are rusty with long disuse. But no matter: the shutter finally opens and the brilliant sunlight streams in. You realize the sun had been there all along, surrounding, embracing the little dark hut. We did not need to beg it to shine. It was its *nature* to shine, and bring radiance, warmth, healing. It had always enveloped the little hut, trying to penetrate its darkness. Slowly (or swiftly) we open the other windows. More light enters. We learn to open the door. The hut is filled with sun and air, and the day will come when we learn to walk freely in and out of the hut.

Prayer is a willingness to learn to say yes to the limitless energy of God within us. Praying is learning to say yes on the physical level, the emotional, the mental. *Not* yes to some anxious image that has been imposed on us by ourselves or others, but yes to the living mystery of the deep self as God increasingly reveals it to us. To pray is to trust that he will bring forth living fruits in due season as we grow—not to force the fruits that we think we ought to have right now. To pray is to give ourselves every day to this healing, releasing light in honest prayer, so that growth will come with grace and not with anxious striving.

In the following chapters I will be discussing this

kind of prayer which enables us to be deeply honest with ourselves as well as with God. This approach lifts the traps of anxious pushing, and releases us to the genuine use of our wings.

It is based on these beliefs:

God loves us as we are. We do not grow to earn his love, but to expand in it. Christ came not to condemn, but to release.

Nothing can come between us and this love of God. Nothing can take us out of his hands.

All energy comes from God alone. In these days of sensational emphasis on the power of Satan and his cohorts, it is well to remember that, though there is indeed evil, there is no *independent source* of evil. Evil is the twisting, misuse, and abuse of energies that originally came from God. All distorted, misused energy can be returned to the one Source for healing.

No soul will be "lost" because of mistaken choices made in this brief life in time and space. There are other levels, other dimensions, other schools of the spirit in which the pilgrim soul may learn what it failed to learn in this world. God is infinitely spacious.

There is nothing innately evil or selfish about *being* a self. If we have not learned to understand, love, and forgive ourselves, neither can we understand and forgive others.

There is no rigid timetable, or program, which determines the rate and manner of our growing and release. Deep wounds, deep powers, must be attended to first. Surface change (bodily healing, outer characteristics) often appears last.

The voice of our true spirit lies deeper than the

voices of emotion or duty. It is that spirit, that self, that needs release.

The light that Christ brought into the world is the same light that lies trapped deep within us. When it is released, by Christ's help we discover to our astonishment that it is our true self, which has always, like the older brother, rejoiced in the Father's home, while the younger brother (our surface self) wandered far away.

It is my belief that the usual way of categorizing prayer—adoration, confession, petition, intercession, commitment—though time-tried and -honored, is *not* the best way for us to seek deep release through prayer. These words impose certain images on us which force us into feelings and actions which do not always rise out of the genuine deep spirit.

The word "adoration" puts the burden on us of producing certain mystical emotions as we approach God. If we do not genuinely have those emotions, we hesitate to approach him. Or we strain to produce them.

"Confession" begs the question, as we turn our eyes to our condition. From the very start we are loaded with guilt. Is there not much more about our human condition than sin and confession?

"Petition" and "intercession" bring up ancient, degrading images of God as one who must be propitiated, explained to, pleaded with. Such concepts lower our trust in him even before we begin.

"Commitment" is a pressuring, programming word. Too many deeply religious people leap to commit themselves to a certain line of action before they have learned to listen to what the deep spirit within is truly saying to them.

I am interested in the kind of prayer which allows God to reveal to us in his own way and time what we truly are, and what we came to do. Releasing prayer, in short.

This gentle cataclysm can occur if we approach prayer in a new way. I have called it the seven Rs:

Relax
Realize
Review
Relinquish
Receive
Release
Radiate

I have tried this approach with several groups I've worked with, and we have found it profoundly releasing. Every one of these steps is well within our power, whatever level of growth we may have reached. They are not dependent on certain emotions. We can approach them just as we really are and really feel. None of them is dependent on certain rigidly laid down rules and techniques. It is a flexible approach and is far more involved with basic attitudes than with rituals and disciplines. It is an approach that is helpful for the beginner in prayer as well as for the experienced. It works on two fronts: deepening awareness of what we are, and, at the same time, deepening release of what we are into the healing light of God. For self-awareness without healing is a depressing morass.

Healing without deepening self-awareness is only incomplete healing.

This approach to prayer, we have found, does not feed us into a self-constructed programming machine, but releases us swiftly into the hands of God who is *alive*.

# 3-Relax and Realize

"You must relax," says the doctor. "Why don't you stop worrying and relax?" say well-meaning friends. Before we know it, relaxation has become another command. A duty. We get tense just thinking about it. Relaxing is not just a matter of willpower and bodily discipline. The roots of tension go far below the surface, and our bodies, obedient servants of our inner selves, act out what we feel.

Because we are distrustful of many things, including ourselves, our bodies become defensive. The face is a tight mask. Hands and feet curl up stiffly. The posture is hunched. The breathing is shallow and quick, and the eyes are strained. Regardless of what we say with words, even in prayer, our bodies say what we really feel: "Go away. I won't let you near me." Our bodies are saying no to God, because inside we feel distrustful or fearful.

Prayer is learning to say yes to God on all the levels of body, emotions, mind, and spirit. This is not learned in a day. Slowly, patiently, we learn to open the windows of our little dark house to the light. The body and the spirit (both manifestations of divine energy) remind each other that there is nothing to fear. They help each other to open and let God in. The body takes a willing, released posture. The spirit expands in the momentarily relaxed body, realizes and reminds the body that God's love surrounds it. The body relaxes further. The spirit can now go deeper and release more of the personality. Thus relaxing and realizing, becoming aware of God's loving presence, the body and the spirit learn together how to say yes to the Cosmic Father.

Relaxing and realizing seems to me a freer, more honest and effective approach to prayer than an emphasis on "adoration." Sometimes genuine feelings of adoration do come as a glorious, spontaneous gift. But to insist, as many prayer manuals do, that we begin with adoration puts a strain and a tension on many people right away. We feel guilty because we are *not* feeling adoring or even worshipful at that moment. Often, if we are honest, we may be feeling nothing but slight boredom, or may be preoccupied with anger, worry, or fatigue.

*It is all right to approach prayer just as we are,* whatever our mood. All God asks is our willingness to be helped. He does not demand particular emotions. Let us be free of all that, and turn toward him our honest self. We can begin to relax and to realize, to allow God's love to enfold us, whatever state we are in, whatever emotion grips us.

There is nothing esoteric or occult about this. No long disciplines are needed. No special diets, strange breathing exercises, or peculiar postures. Five or ten minutes and a reasonably quite place to sit are all that is needed.

Take the tense body, the clamoring emotions, and confused mind over to the chair. Sit down with feet on the floor, and the palms open in the lap. Remind the body that it is to be something like a TV antenna "transforming the wavelength of Heaven into the wavelength of earth," as one scientist has put it. Or, picture the body as an electric cord with the energy of light streaming through it. Or if these seem too mechanical, picture the body as a strong limb of a deep-rooted tree, allowing the vital nourishment of the tree to stream through it. Remind the body that its very cells, all its organs, will share in this divine interchange. The body can best cooperate in this by being straight, alert, well grounded, expectant.

Check the muscles of the hands and feet. Let them smooth out. How about the face? Is there a tight society plaster mask on it? Let it melt as if a hand gently sponged it with a warm cloth. Let the muscles around the mouth and eyes and scalp go limp. No one is looking at us now except the One who already knows what we really look like.

Now breathe slowly and deeply, letting the whole chest expand. Breathe out even more slowly, as fully as possible. Do this several times. This stretches and relaxes the cramped muscles around the lungs, and fills the grateful blood vessels with oxygen. Now let the breathing become natural, slow, and light.

The body has now done its initial part and is able now to hear what the mind and the spirit say. Our problems and disturbed emotions are still present, of course. Tell them gently that they will have their say and be fully heard in a few moments. But first comes the *realizing* of the presence of him who is with us.

There are many ways of realizing his presence. I personally find that the most helpful is to visualize a warm, white, radiant light surrounding me. It is a fact that the light of the healing Christ exists and permeates and acts whether or not we are aware of it. Some prefer to picture the light as the whiteness of a blazing young sun. Others find that picture too bright, too blinding. They prefer to think of a deep, rich gold which soothes as well as burns. Some prefer the freshness and healing quality of green, or the mystery of blue. God in his mercy gives himself to us in any way we can best take him, just as white light can be filtered through a prism and manifest itself as many colors. (His very incarnation in his Son, Jesus, was a filtering mercy. He did not overwhelm us with his unshielded power and reality.)

Some people don't like the picture of light alone in their prayers. I had a conversation once with a gentle, beautiful person who said the constant visualizing of light per se made her feel hot and uncomfortable. Her natural inner sanctuary was a garden, with green ferns, moss, vines, and a trickling stream. How tyrannical it would be to try to brainwash her out of her garden onto some sunswept mountain! We must each find the inner place where we are most relaxed, most aware of the surrounding mercy of our Maker.

Some prefer to center on a significant symbol, such as a slowly opening flower, or a deep-rooted, fruitful tree. Some prefer to picture Jesus Christ himself, in human form, standing in the room before them.

Perhaps you don't want to use a picture or symbol at all. Perhaps you prefer to use the vibration of sound rather than sight. You can say aloud or mentally a few words that bring to you an immediate awareness of divine love. It can be from Scriptures or a hymn— but that is not necessary. Any words will do that in a brief, natural form suggest the healing presence:

> "Christ, you are the vine, I am the branch."
> "Christ is risen!"
> "Around us are the everlasting arms."
> "Our God is a consuming fire."
> "The thought of thee is mightier far
>    Than sin and pain and sorrow are."
> "God, nothing can separate me from you."
> "Breathe on me, Breath of God."

Words such as these can be repeated aloud several times, slowly and thoughtfully. It is a wonderful way for the body to participate in the realizing of God's presence.

Perhaps you are a person who prefers to say or picture *nothing*. This is quite all right. Merely compose the body as suggested, and ask God to work on you, body and mind, according to his will. This sounds very dry, unimaginative, and unemotional, but actually it is a prayer of the profoundest kind of trust and power. When we leave the whole thing in his hands, the results are surprising.

We need not use the same approach every day.

Some days we may wish to picture light, or some scene or symbol. Other days we may wish to speak aloud, or merely affirm his presence and wait expectantly. We may latch onto one way that is especially helpful for many months, and then find that we are growing into a new way or method. Our chosen method must not become a trap itself. If any mental imagery becomes confining, monotonous, unrefreshing, that is a warning sign that we have outgrown it. We must then allow our deep unfolding self to suggest a new way.

Whatever method of realization develops, let it include these releasing thoughts:

> God is here.
> He surrounds and understands all that I am—on all levels.
> He loves me forever. He will never give up in disgust.
> At this very moment he is helping me grow and be healed.
> He is not hurrying or forcing me.
> Only part of me is now really willing. Someday, all of me will be willing.
> He is here.

Is the body listening? Let it reflect back the calm expectancy of the spirit as a quiet lake reflects the majesty of the mountain.

Now we are relaxed and realizing. Even if we did only this for five or ten minutes a day, our lives would be profoundly changed.

*But this is only the first step into prayer that releases!*

MISERICORDIAS DOMINI · IN ETERNVM CANTABO

B.V. TERESA DE JESV

ANNO SVÆ
ÆTATIS
LXI
A SALVTIS
1576

STAB. L. SALOMONE - ROMA

*teresa de jesus*

# 4-Review and Relinquish

Now the quiet, cleansed body and spirit can turn to the problems of the emotions. They have been relaxed temporarily, but they are still there. They belong to us. They are our children and we are responsible for them. We cannot shove them into a dark closet and pretend they do not exist.

Of all illnesses, the worst come from the emotions which we either pretend do not exist or allow to take over our whole being like a cancer on the rampage. Most of us who are trying to grow in Christ fall into the trap of pretending our feelings do not exist. We have been told so often, in so many prayer manuals, that we must get rid of fear, anger, and all "negative" emotions. We have been told that anger can destroy us and our brother. We have been told that fear will block the great work of God through us. We have been told that anxiety and worry are a shameful lack of faith.

*We have become afraid of our fear! We worry about our worry! We get angry with ourselves for feeling anger!* We are sure that the ideal Christian we are trying to imitate never feels that way. So because we are trying to be that ideal Christian, when these feelings arise, we become ashamed, guilty, panicky. We try to *pretend* that we are full of joy, trust and confidence—and call this pretense "faith." Christians have *no right* to negative emotions, we have been told. The results of this pretense and imitation can be disastrous.

I knew a man slowly dying of a blood ailment. He had been for years an active Christian leader and much interested in healing prayer. When told he had this serious illness, he never showed any fear or worry, and never admitted he felt any. Always he presented a face of smiling confidence to his friends—and to himself. He allowed only his hopeful, courageous feelings to show themselves. This, he had been taught to believe, was the only way a Christian could receive healing. Perfect faith was his ideal and his goal. Slowly and steadily his health failed, and about a month before his death he suddenly went into a severe nervous breakdown. All his unadmitted feelings of fear and doubt rushed to the surface and overwhelmed him. He thought this meant that he was not a real Christian— that he was letting God down. After some days of dreadful darkness, slowly he came to realize that, far from letting God down by his fears and lack of faith, he was at last allowing his *full* self as a person to come forth to the Great Healer. He finally allowed God to embrace and heal these inner, real feelings. It was the beginning of a far deeper faith than he had ever known, for he was no longer trying to push positive feelings on himself. He came to God, just as he was. His body died without pain, and his spirit went on without fear to the next great step of growing.

I learned much from this man. I learned that we need not be afraid of our feelings, even the so-called negative feelings, so long as we face them fully, *review* them, and then *relinquish* them. That is, look at them for what they are, and turn them over to the Great Physician for healing.

This is the step of prayer ordinarily called "confession"—which, like "adoration" is a very limited category. Adoration is only one part of a deep *realizing*. Confession is only one part of a deep *reviewing*. Confession means facing a definite, deliberate sin. By "sin" I mean any act or word which deliberately tries to belittle or destroy the well-being, freedom, and dignity of our own or another's deep self. But there is so much more within us to review and look at, besides sin. There are deep-rooted limitations and blocks which are not deliberate at all. There are also positive fruits of growth which must be reviewed and rejoiced over. There are involuntary mistaken choices and unintentional wanderings from the true self. There are unresolved problems and honest bewilderment. There is deep involvement with the lives and feelings of others. All this needs to be looked at. To call all this "sin," needing "confession," loads us with new burdens of meaningless guilt.

Thus, I use a word like "review," which includes all these other aspects of ourselves as well as sin.

To begin our review of ourselves, let us first know this: *God never blames us for a feeling. A feeling is not a sin. It is a symptom.* No matter what the feeling itself is—whether anger, fear, doubt, loneliness, envy, lust, frustration, impatience—by itself, as a feeling, it is not sin. We need only fear our feelings if they are driven down into the basement of our personalities and ignored (for then they spread like poison through our whole system), *or* if they are allowed to disrupt our whole lives and injure us or others.

But the prayer that releases, honest prayer, can release us from either of those two destructive situations.

This is done by allowing each acute or chronic feeling to step forward at this point in our praying. *Let it come forth as your little injured child.* Suppose it is anger that steps forth first: anger at some loved one, hatred of an enemy, or maybe deep anger at God. It shocks a Christian to look at this child called anger. But it is your child. It came, not from some devil who is tempting you, but from some deep-down, God-given *energy* which was once beautiful, but which has been badly hurt and disfigured somehow.

Look down at the furious little face. It is part of you. Don't hush it down. Let it speak and say what it feels. *Listen* to what it says. Perhaps it will say in modern language what the Psalmist said long ago:

I hate the company of evildoers,
    and I will not sit with the wicked. (Ps. 26:5)

Let them be turned back and brought to dishonor
    who desire my hurt. (Ps. 40:14)

I was envious of the arrogant,
    when I saw the prosperity of the wicked. . . .
Always at ease, they increase in riches.
All in vain have I kept my heart clean. (Ps. 73:3, 12-13)

34

God does not hate you because you are expressing your anger. Rather, it is a great sign of trust on your part that you are letting it out in his loving presence.

Listen, in his presence, to what your anger is saying in whatever language it chooses to say it in. See if it is arising from a genuine problem or situation which is truly harmful to you. Or is it an unrealistic anger lashing out at others rather than facing the real issue? Then mentally pick up your child, anger, in your arms and go with it into God's healing sunlight. Hold it in the light. Picture God's hands taking the anger and the problem from you. *Relinquish* it to him. Then let the deep, beautiful energy (which had become anger) be returned to you healed.

All energy is from God and can never be destroyed. But it can be twisted and injured, and needs to be relinquished to the source of all energy for healing.

Is your problem fear? Call that child forth. It needs cherishing and comforting. There is nothing shameful or unchristian about feeling fear. Jesus felt great fear in Gethsemane. So did the Psalmist:

My God, my God, why has thou forsaken me?
Why art thou so far from helping me? . . .
I am poured out like water . . .
my strength is dried up. (Ps. 22:1, 14)

In the night my hand is stretched out . . .
my soul refuses to be comforted. . . .
I meditate, and my spirit faints. . . .
I am so troubled that I cannot speak. (Ps. 77:2-4)

Are we ashamed of our anxiety about old age or illness? The Psalmist felt it too:

> Do not cast me off in the time of old age;
>> forsake me not when my strength is spent.
>>> (Ps. 71:9)

Are we afraid of God himself? Do we fear that he is condemning or punishing us?

> My flesh trembles for fear of thee,
>> and I am afraid of thy judgments.
>>> (Ps. 119:120)

> Why dost thou stand afar off, O Lord?
> Why dost thou hide thyself in times of trouble?
>> (Ps. 10:1)

Many, many of us are deeply afraid of God, without realizing it. Though we are taught to call him a God of love and mercy, often we are afraid that he is really an angry, punishing father, jealous of any good times we have, swift to bring us to our "just deserts." He knows that often we have this fear, and that often we are distrustful.

This does not make him angry. It will not block his work of healing through us, so long as we face the feeling and hold it up, relinquish it to his hands for healing:

"God, though I know you are loving and merciful and want good for me, just the same there is a large part of me which is afraid and doesn't trust you. At this moment, this part of me is crying with fear deep down inside."

This is a prayer of trustful honesty. It may be all that is needed to *un*block the work he tries to do through us!

Listen and look at this panicky child of yours called fear. It, too, has come from some beautiful energy within which was wounded, perhaps long ago. Longer ago than you can consciously remember. This is a part of you that does *not* need more scolding, moralizing, punishing. It needs cradling and healing. *God does not hate your fear.* Every day relinquish it again to his hands. Bring your child every day to this radiant, warm light, and hold it there lovingly for several minutes. If new layers of fear are revealed, bring them too. He is greater than our fears. He is infinitely deeper than our anxiety, no matter how deeply that anxiety is rooted.

This healing is seldom accomplished quickly. It may take many months, for we must never hurry or push the process. This kind of prayer is not compulsive or hurried. We don't need to dredge things up. Rather we are to keep an open willingness to look at whatever emerges as we grow. God won't make us look at more than we can bear at any one time. Next year we will be looking with tenderness and understanding at fears that we could not bear to face this year.

This loving acceptance and relinquishment to God's light can be practiced in little ways through the day. A woman recently became aware that she was a true hypochrondriac. She was always anticipating the worst in every symptom in herself or her family. The way she made the most of every little cold, backache, stomach upset, every little risk her perfectly normal children took, was eating into the full, joyous living she wanted.

At first when she realized her fearfulness, she condemned it as a sin, and promised herself never to worry anymore about anything. She tried to force herself into optimism, which merely added extra strain, tension, guilt.

Then she learned the genuine release of honest prayer. She took out her tense little child, worry, and gave it a long look. She admitted that it existed and came from some deep level within her. Then she admitted that she didn't have any idea at all how to heal this worry. All her good resolutions had got her nowhere. She held her worried self in God's light, and asked him to take over this problem and this wounded energy. She asked his light to penetrate to the levels of the subconscious self where rested the roots of the problem. Knowing that prayer is energy released, she knew that the work had begun, even though she felt nothing as yet. She waited with expectant interest to see how the healing would take place.

During the day she practiced this relinquishment with *little* worries, knowing that she would not have 100 percent faith all at once. When her children took small risks, instead of shouting anxiously, "Look out! Be careful!" or on the other hand merely forcing herself to watch with a strained, false smile and inner torture, she would silently admit that she was anxious. Then she would turn over her worried self and her active children to the white light of God's protection.

When she awoke in the morning with a headache and a stuffy nose, she would not immediately cancel all her appointments for the week and begin swallowing antibiotics, nor would she force herself to ignore her symptoms, muttering grimly, "Christians mustn't feel worried or sick." She would honestly admit that she felt an illness creeping up on her, and then place the whole issue in God's hands (while at the same time using ordinary commonsense measures to help her body resist the germs). If visions of weeks in bed rose to scare her, she would admit she felt real fear, and again hold it in God's light.

Slowly, as time went on, she got more used to admitting how she really felt. She became less afraid of her fear, knowing it could not in itself seriously block God's work in her or through her. Little by little the iron grip of her anxiety relaxed. Her instinctive, shrinking defensiveness was slowly replaced by trustfulness. *No longer did she depend on her willpower or idealism to force this trust. The trust welled up from within as she was increasingly healed within.*

Then, as so often happens, not only did her worries fade away, but so did the many physical symptoms that had plagued her so long. She has not had a cold for two years (though in the early stages of her growing trust she had as many as ever). As her fear of life has lessened, not only she but her whole family is released to greater fullness of life.

Let the other emotions stand forth. Whether it is grief, or envy, or desire, or compulsive perfectionism, take it like a child in your arms, a child that was once beautiful. Listen to what it says, fully, and then carry it into the light. Do the same with a painful *memory*.

If there is a problem that you cannot solve, give it a long, thoughtful look, admit you cannot solve it, and hold it in God's light and watch expectantly for guidance.

The beautiful, creative emotions also, and the fruits of growing and loving—these, too, we review. They are our joyous, healthy children. Let them speak their happiness or confidence. Look fully at their lovely reality, and lift them in the light with thanksgiving, praying that they remain healthy and beautiful. Our normal children need loving attention as well as our wounded ones.

This kind of released praying takes us out of the realm of God's judgment and our guilt, God's orders and our obedience. It takes us out of set laws and rigid requirements for a Christian personality. It puts us into a new relationship, a new dimension of spontaneity and healing.

*Do not fear that such praying will leave you just where you are. On the contrary, you will change more swiftly than ever before. But the change will come from within as a release, not be imposed from without as a law. And the change may be unexpected, and not at all as we had formerly visualized.*

This is also true of the aspect of review which we call confession. Yes, there is indeed a place for confession and review of sin. But the sin is not the *feeling*. The sin is an *act* which arose when our child, the emotion, was allowed to get out of control, and to hurt the other children within us. Or if it has been allowed to hurt the child within someone else. It is not the anger which we confess as sin, but the *action* of contempt and hurtfulness: the malicious or sarcastic word, the lifted eyebrow behind someone's back, the sneering putdown to make another feel small. Or the inner or outer refusal to let the other person be what he wants to be. The closing of the door against awareness of the mystery and essential goodness of the other person. The use of him for our own ends, riding roughshod over his freedom of decision.

We sin against ourselves in the same way. We crush down some part of ourself which has a right to exist and to be heard. For example, we sin against ourselves if we harshly criticize something in ourselves which has been momentarily lazy, weak, frivolous, desirous, without asking *why* that part of us exists and what important thing it might be trying to express.

I always find that those who are most coldly critical and repressive of others have first of all treated *themselves* that way. I have known men and women who were suspicious of the gentleness and tenderness within themselves, thinking it weakness. So they had forced down the tender side and devoted themselves to the development of ruthless, efficient power.

Conversely, I knew the son of such a man, who grew up so suspicious of efficiency and power (which he felt had ruined his father's life) that he cultivated *only* emotional tenderness and sensitivity in his own life, and forced down much of his own genuine gift for powerful, creative action. He thought he was free. But actually he was as repressed as his father! Just as the father feared to let himself love warmly and give expression to a deep artistic nature, so the son feared to get his roots into *any* way of life or make any firm decisions about anything.

Thus we sin against ourselves, as well as against

others, when we shut the door, refuse to listen, manipulate, force, degrade.

We can look at what we have done (and often done in the name of goodness or religion) and can pray with honesty:

"Yes, that is part of me too. I did not merely feel anger. I reached out and struck hurtfully at the divine energy—God's own face. I tried to hurt and destroy something, a mystery which I did not understand. I took God's own energy, and used it against him. I used someone else, without reverence for his freedom and growth."

The Scriptures tell us:

Be angry, but sin not;
   commune with your own hearts on your beds,
      and be silent. (Ps. 4:4)

What a releasing and healing counsel! The feeling of anger will often arise at ourselves or at our brother. But that does not necessarily lead to sin. We have a split second of choice, of free will, as we face the anger. We can either permit our child, the anger, to become a juvenile delinquent, stamping down our other children of tenderness and gentleness, reaching out to hurt and belittle the other person. Or we can offer up the whole surging energy we feel to God's light, refusing to let it become an instrument of hurtfulness:

"Take it over, Christ, this power of anger (or jealousy, or fear, or desire). Use this deep energy according to the radiance of your will."

This prayer can be used at any moment of the day as our feelings threaten to engulf us and lead us to sin.

Do not think that God will answer this prayer by leading us back to the shell of *non*-feeling. Quite the contrary. As we grow in energy and power in Christ, so will many deep feelings grow. We may experience *deeper* anger, *deeper* hurt, *deeper* desires and longings, because we will be growing more aware in every way. God does not administer anesthetics. But our deep, vivid feelings will no longer control or intimidate us. We will have learned, relaxed in God's presence, to deal with them compassionately. We will have learned that the energies they represent are never destroyed, but are transformed. The anger that fills us so that we bang doors, crash through housework, shout, will still surge up in us, but with a different manifestation altogether. We will have learned where to turn for healing.

Review and relinquish. This is the point of pain and joy in which the bird is released from the wire, the fruit tree allows itself to produce its own fruit, and the boarded-up windows are uncovered. The work of release moves deeper.

> See what is there.
> Accept with compassion what is there.
> Hold that which you see in God's radiant light.
> Let the nature and timing of the change rest in his hands.

43

# 5-Receive

It is hard to learn to receive. We prefer to act, to do something, to express something, to say something, to give or show something. That is much easier than receiving what someone else is trying to say, show, do, give. I heard it said cynically of a woman, "She is so busy giving herself out to others, she no time to take anyone else in."

In one of his books, C. S. Lewis remembers how for several days he had a constant feeling that God was trying to tell him something. He wondered guiltily what he had left undone, and stepped up his good works and worship. Finally one day it came to him, with surprise, that God was saying, "Relax. Be still. I want to *give* you something!"

This is precisely the point where both prayer and human relationships break down. I think there are two main reasons. First, it takes some energy, patience, and disciplined willingness to set aside what we are doing and to *listen* and receive. To listen deeply—not only to what is being said, but to what is being implied. It is hard to listen to what our deep self is saying. Perhaps even harder than to listen to what our emotions are saying. It takes even more patient willingness to receive deeply what is being offered. And our deep self, through which speaks the voice of God, is always offering that which we need.

Second, we fear that if we listen and receive we are admitting weakness and dependence. A person who shows off is really saying, "I am afraid I am really nothing important. I must hurry to put forward what little I have before the others find me out!"

This is one of the main reasons why both human relationships and prayer do not go deeper and become more effective for us. In prayer, up to this point we have been pretty active. There have been things for us to do. We have put ourselves into a state of *relaxation*. We have put ourselves into *realization* by picturing the light of God around us. We have *reviewed* what is within by calling forth our emotions, and dealing with them compassionately, as children. Even the *relinquishment* has taken action on our part as we take these wounded children and place them in the healing hands. Thus far, it has been a flowing out to God as far as our conscious awareness is concerned (though already deep healing and receiving is going on in the subconscious).

But now comes the moment for the *conscious* self to listen deeply and receive deeply. This takes practice.

What is God saying to us now through our deep self? What are the signals? What is the gift he is trying to give at this very moment?

Here is a helpful picture which explains this moment. Picture yourself in the garden, about to do some work. You pull your gardening glove over your hand,

and pick up a tool. Now is the moment for the hand to receive the signals, the purpose, the guidance, and the energy from the brain and the rest of the body. But suppose the hand is unable, for some reason, to receive or interpret the brain signals? Or suppose it is unable to receive energy from the nerve impulses or the circulation of the blood? It would remain inert and paralyzed. Or it would move with random purposelessness. If the hand had a kind of conscious awareness of its own, it would be wondering, "What am I doing here? What is this glove? This tool? What did I come here to do? Why can't I do it?"

The plight of this semiparalyzed hand is the plight of most of us in this world. We came here to do and to be something. We have sheathed ourselves in space, time, and flesh. We have picked up the tool of a body and a brain. We appear to be ready for the real work. But most of the communication has broken down between our surface, conscious selves and that deep self which we call the spirit. So we live out our life in space, time, and the flesh, puzzled, random, weak, or even half-paralyzed, dimly remembering or guessing why we came. Just as the hand could not hear the mind, so the surface, conscious self cannot hear the spirit.

The prayer of receiving is one of the swiftest, deepest ways of restoring communication. Our deep selves, our spirits, are always in the presence of God. Even the wickedest man or woman always has that light burning within, "the true light that enlightens every man," but has closed most of the doors of his conscious and subconscious self against it.

The listening, the receiving, should usually come after the compassionate reviewing because otherwise our emotions, longings, needs can easily block the voice of the deep self, much as some local interference blocks the radio or TV reception.

Relax the body again, taking a few deep, calm breaths. Keep the hands open as a gesture of receiving. Remind yourself quietly that God, who has stilled our bodies, who is healing our wounds of memory and emotion, now wishes to speak directly to our conscious selves.

His voice will not be the voice of our turbulent emotions. Take care that you do not think *his* voice is that anger, pride, frustration, or possessiveness you may have been feeling. Those voices, which sound so authoritative, are those hurt children of ours that need healing.

Nor is his voice always the same as that voice which we usually call our "conscience" or "duty." Too often what we think is the command of God is only the expectations of our parents, our church, our neighbors, our culture, or our perfectionist selves trying to imitate that "perfect" Christian out there. For many years, I thought God's voice *was* that voice within me which sternly told my feelings to be quiet or to go away. It took me a long time to realize that it wasn't God at all, but only a repressive, muscle-bound part of my own self, trying to be dictator over the rest of me!

So now listen deeper than the voice of feelings and the voice of "duty." What is the *real* spirit saying? Drop deliberate pictures or thoughts. Let a gentle sponge wipe the mind clear. Remain silent and expectant.

For most of us God's voice will not come as words which we hear or see, though for some it may. For many of us it comes as an inner picture or symbol. A friend of mine, who was very tired, received during the listening part of her prayer the spontaneous image of a glass held under a sparkling fountain of water, which not only filled the glass, but ran over the sides. If she had listened to her *emotions* as if they were God, instead of tired children, she would have thought God was saying," Drop all your work. You've made a mistake in thinking you can do it. You're just plain weak and neurotic." Or if she had mistaken the typical voice of *duty* for the voice of God, she would have thought he was saying, "Don't be so lazy. Stop pitying yourself. Get up and work harder, Never mind how you feel." But because she had learned that God does not speak in these ways, she waited, receptive, open, expectant. And slowly, clearly, lovingly from the depths came that beautiful symbol of the "cup running over." She knew God was saying, "Yes, you are tired. You need refreshment that only I can give before you go back to work. And then your beautiful energy will be not only filling your own cup, but brimming over to refresh others."

Perhaps his voice of guidance will come in the sudden understanding of a dream we have had many times over the years. Dreams can be most helpful if we realize that the people and places we dream about are usually parts of ourselves that the spirit explores and seeks to heal.

The guidance may come as a new idea, a new thought, a new line of action suggested which had not occurred to us before.

We may suddenly remember some incident or some person, and this memory will shed light on the present.

The gift and the message may be the beginning of a hopefulness and peace and power which we had never felt before. Perhaps we do not see the way clearly yet, but that no longer depresses us. It is as if a heavy fog were lifting, and soon the sun will break through and the path lie clearly ahead.

God's voice may be the sense of being deeply nourished and cared for. There are many people who are so psychically sensitive and open to others that they quickly become exhausted. They have not learned to put themselves under Christ's protective light before intercessory prayer or counseling, and they have come to the end of their own energy. As a result, they frequently go into physical prostration, suffering from nightmares, headaches, inability to sleep, nervous symptoms of all kinds. Often they feel guilty about this, especially if they are prayer leaders or counselors to others. What we need when we get in such a state (after we have checked that there is nothing organically wrong) is to put ourselves quite deliberately into a spiritual "hospital bed" and let ourselves be cared for by the Divine Physician. Alert a prayer group or a praying friend to your problem. Ask for special help to be channeled by them to you for a few days. Drop intercessory prayer for those few days, especially prayer for those who are undergoing emotional problems. (Don't feel guilty about this. You are not copping out or "laying down your cross." You will return to this vocation of helping and healing others with renewed power when you are replenished.) Picture yourself actually having a blood transfusion if that is helpful. Something like that is going on. If that brings up negative associations picture yourself, as in the Twenty-Third Psalm, lying down in soft green grass beside a quiet lake. Or think of yourself as being held in the hand of God, lying down on the hand, not even trying to hold on. Just being held. In short, make your praying time for several days a *receiving* time—but receiving of healing only, not ideas for new lines of action.

Whatever way we receive from God, we may only slightly or dimly receive it at first. Few of us experience a suddenly wide-flung door with floods of light pouring in. For most of us, the long shut door to our inner spirit will open slowly and hesitatingly, admitting at first just a little guidance and help and understanding. But as our experience and trust grow, each day it will open wider. God will not be irritated at our slowness. He understands that it takes a while for life to flow back into the paralyzed hand.

But however it comes, by words, symbols, pictures, dreams, memories, healing, we will know it to be the true voice of God by certain signs.

It never comes with compulsion or force. God's voice and gifts leave us *free*. Beware of inner voices or guidance which say, "You've got to . . ." "You must . . ." "Obey or else . . ." The true Spirit speaks to us as the bridegroom who opens his arms, not the law-enforcement agent hauling us into court. The Christ *knocks* at our door, calling us to festival and celebration. He doesn't bash it down or force the lock.

It comes with *meaning*. When we hear it or perceive it, the jigsaw puzzle of our lives begins to take shape and pattern. Things begin to make sense. What we see or hear becomes self-evident.

It seems *natural* and *spontaneous*. What we see or hear or feel will seem like homecoming. Like part of ourselves. Perhaps a long forgotten home or a neglected part, but still part of what we *are*. We seem to recognize it, and there will be no awkwardness or forced grace.

It is *surprising* as well as natural. It never comes as the same boring old thing. Even if the line of action suggested is not a new one to us, it will be suggested in a new and refreshing way. We will feel, "I never thought of it in *that* way before!" And often the line of action will be a new one altogether. New to our conscious self, that is.

It will come with *joy*. Even when a difficult or painful way is suggested to us, if it is suggested by God, it will be shot through with joy as it was with Jesus "who for the joy that was set before him endured the cross." Beware of picking up crosses which do not bring with them that joy. They are not the cross meant for us!

It will come with *power*. No weak, limp Spirit stands on the other side of that door. Once we are willing to open the door, God's energy will flood our lives. If he offers a way that demands strength of us, he gives us that strength in the same moment. Beware of any way that leaves you struggling feebly in your own willpower and good intentions.

It will come with *fruitfulness*. When we are listening to the true voice of the Spirit, there will be real healings, real changes, creative actions, new relationships. Not right away, perhaps. Some of us need deep inner healing and nourishment before the changes appear outwardly. But sooner or later the fruits *will* appear in our lives (though they may not be the ones expected). If we are floundering in continual failure and frustration, it is probable that we are not misunderstood martyrs, but rather that we have not been hearing what God is really saying to us. It is probable that we have been listening only to the voices of unhealed emotions or the voice of duty (as others interpret it for us).

Above all, the voice and gift of God bring us to the step of *release*.

# 6-Release

Just what is it that is increasingly released as we grow in this relaxed kind of prayer? It is our true self. It is the real "I" which is forever deathless in the light of the Father. Unfortunately such words as "spirit" and "soul" have come to have a vague, misty quality. Such words and concepts as "he passed on" or "our loved ones hovering near us" reinforce this murky, unreal feeling about our "spirits."

Theologians call it the "Image of God." St. Paul spoke of the "celestial body." Some religious groups call it a "body of light." But whatever we call it, this deathless self, it is real, radiant, powerful, and unique. It is full of light and health. We do not create it through prayer and good deeds; it already exists. It is not handed to use when we go to Heaven. We already dwell in it, though most of us are only dimly aware of it.

It is this "self" which has put on the glove of flesh and blood for adventure in this world. After the glove is removed through physical death, it will continue its adventure through the many dimensions ("mansions") of God's creation.

What shape has it? What form? It doesn't matter. We can probably experience any form we wish after we have learned to open all the doors of our Father's house, and feel at home in all the rooms. The day will come when our "self" is at ease in all parts of the universe, visible and invisible.

It is this self of light from which the physical cells take directly their daily energy and health. It is this deep self which looks with loving compassion on our many emotions and our childlike aspects. It is this deep spirit which enters into colors and sounds with a vividness and poignance that we can hardly imagine. As our daily, *conscious* self joins more fully with the deep self, then in daily life we will become more aware of colors, sounds, fragrance, touch, taste. (The members of our prayer group have noticed how the colors of the carpet beneath our feet seem to leap out vividly after a half-hour of prayer and silent meditation. And how poignantly sing the birds outside the window!)

Far from being vague and ethereal, the self of light enters profoundly into the five senses, filling and fulfilling them with its own vast energy. But even as it enters lovingly into the world of matter, it is also in authority over it, even as the mythic Adam was in loving authority over his Garden of Eden.

Sexual awareness, also, will be more keen. This startles many people growing spiritually who had thought *that* part of awareness would somehow just go away. Not at all. That, too, was part of the original beauty of man's aware spirit in Eden, according to God's will.

54

The powerful, magnetic attraction to other people will grow, even as all the other energies and perceptions will grow as the inner spirit is released. We will especially feel this attraction to those with whom we recognize a spiritual kinship. This need not disturb us. We need not feel guilty because we are more, not less, aware of male and female. It is something to rejoice in as a very real sign of the growing release of the spirit. We can enjoy the awareness as part of the "salt" of daily life. We can welcome it as a real part of the mystery and beauty of another individual.

But we do not need to let this released perception *master* us. The sexual energy is only one among many, and must not be allowed to take command over all the other energies within. For then we will be trapped, not free. We must allow many energies to develop, as part of the supreme cosmic energy beginning to sweep so fully through us.

We human beings—especially we *religious* human beings—have a strange way of singling out one special energy, such as the sexual, and worshiping it as a supreme divinity, or despising and stamping on it as if it were created by Lucifer. Of course, either extreme is a destructive misunderstanding. *All* energies are ultimately from God, the one Source, the one Creator. But many of them have been badly misused and distorted, and must be held in the supreme light for healing. So don't be afraid of these deep magnetic feelings. They are part of God's supreme energy. If they seem to be getting out of balance, assuming mastery over you in a destructive way, then relinquish them to God's light for healing. He will return them to you, still strong, but channeled creatively, in harmony with the rest of your personality.

The *psychic* awareness is another great energy which will be released as our spirit takes command. This, like the sexual energy, has been much misunderstood and abused. It has been either worshiped or despised and feared. I have noticed sadly, in recent years, a serious polarization over psychic development taking place. On the one hand, many evangelical charismatic Christian groups have become extremely suspicious of *anything* that appears psychic. Telepathic and clairvoyant experiments are frowned on. *Any* attempt at communication with spirits, who live now in other dimensions, no matter how spontaneous and innocent it is, is considered extremely dangerous. Some evangelical leaders go so far as to say that *all* forms of extrasensory perception are from the devil, and thus by nature evil.

On the other hand, there are certainly many occult groups who elevate the psychic perception into a position of near divinity. There are many who venture with foolhardy rashness into trances, out-of-the-body experiences, communication with spirits, without the least idea how to protect themselves first with Christ's light. To venture into psychic dimensions out of mere curiosity, greed, or desire for power over others, is as dangerous as walking alone and unprotected down the dark streets of a great city.

So we have this polarization: on the one hand, rigid, intolerant strictures against psychic development, and on the other, foolish worship and abuse of it. Sometimes one finds these extremes in one person.

Recently I read an autobiography, much in circulation now, written by a former spiritualist medium. For the first half of his life, he devoted all his time and energy to psychic growth and communication, ignoring, it seems to me, any kind of wise protection against danger, any kind of sensible discrimination between the spirits. Then he became converted to a certain type of Christianity, and now all things psychic, even the spontaneous, wise, and innocent, are in his eyes mere disguises of Satan's power. He seems to me similar to a person who, having made a foolish and unhappy marriage, is now against *all* marriage, for himself or others.

The point is that psychic power, like sexual energy, is ultimately from God, part of his supreme energy. As our deep spirit is fully released, psychic awareness is usually far more in evidence. We will be far more aware of thought communication with others. We will sense when they need to be prayed for. We will sometimes be able to see or hear at a distance without the use of our physical eyes or ears. Sometimes we will be aware, dimly or keenly, of the presence of someone who has died. Sometimes we may find ourselves spontaneously outside the physical body, able to move around and make contact with others. All this is quite normal. It shows that our personalities are not limited by space, time, and the five senses, and as our spirit is released, it will often act through these invisible or psychic "senses." The Bible, as well as the scriptures of all the great religions, is full of such incidents, often with reference to people of great holiness. These phenoma are nothing to be feared—or worshiped.

But if the psychic energy has been misused and abused, if it has begun to hurt us or others, or to limit our growth, this means that we have allowed that energy to get out of balance. It will not be destroyed, but it must be submitted to God's light for healing. Some *may* find that they have to avoid deliberate psychic acts themselves (without condemning it for others), just as an alcoholic must not take even one glass of light wine. Most of us, I believe, would do well *not* to deliberately set out to develop psychic ability, and above all *not* to force it. But if *spontaneous* awareness develops as we grow in prayer, then let us accept it as a natural thing, with calmness and gratitude, placing ourselves always in Christ's white protecting light (as we should do with any adventure of our energy) and using it for good.

Other abilities and energies will come forth as the spirit within is released, all kinds of gifts and powers. Some may be familiar to us. Others may be totally new. We may discover that we are healers. We might see come forth a power for speaking or writing or organizing. We might experience a compassionate perception which means we are counselors. We might find a radiant creative power which desires to express itself through music, singing, painting, dancing. There may leap alive within us a burning wish to lay hold of some dark, cancerous problem in this world and help heal it. Or we may find a joyous ability to make a releasing, peaceful home and neighborhood.

We cannot tell what beautiful thing will come forth as our spirits are released. That is why I prefer the word "release" to that of "commitment." The word, "commitment" is too often associated with a programming from the outside before the person has had time to listen to what his deep spirit is really saying. Once our true being is released there will be no need for formal commitment. We will *know* who we are and why we have come into life.

I am particularly sorry when I see young people who are rushed into a lifelong pledge to some special line of Christian action out of group emotion or a compulsive sense of duty. The deep springs of the spirit are not usually quickly revealed. The young person can give himself to the living Christ—and then keep an open mind and heart to what great gifts and energies that Christ will reveal to him. If in the first burst of emotion he has committed himself to be a minister, missionary, or social worker, and then later he discovers that God has given him far more the abilities of a businessman, artist, or scientist, he may have quite a struggle to release himself from a sense of guilt that he has "laid down the cross' or "taken his hand from the plow." The real problem is that he did not take enough time of relaxed, receptive thought and prayer to discover what was the *real* plow or cross for him.

There is nothing passive about this kind of releasing prayer. Some people misunderstand this. I recall that one young man I was counseling thought for a long time that this way of praying meant that one makes no decisions and takes no action. He thought I was recommending floating on the waves of the spirit like seaweed.

Naturally we will make decisions. Naturally we will

take action. We came into the world to do just this. But the *creative* action will only be possible when we have listened to what our real spirit is saying in our depths. The word "resolve" does not just mean making up one's mind to do something. It means that something has taken shape, or fallen into its proper place. When the pattern of our life has truly taken shape and the true gifts of the spirit come forth, we will know what we are to do, and the power to do it will be given along with the knowing.

So each day, at this point of our prayer, let us pray that what is genuinely right for us be increasingly revealed with its attendant joyful power. Let us pray that what is *not* right for us at this point be crowded out as a superfluous, unfitting thing as the spirit fills our lives, or that it be healed. We cannot always decide as rigid rules what is wrong for us. What may be an expanding experience for you right now, may become a serious limitation to your spiritual growth and harmony later on.

As a rather strange example, I knew a man who learned some early lessons of relaxation, receptivity, and appreciation of beauty through wine-drinking. It was not a question of riotous drunkenness. He never once became drunk. But he had been a compulsive person, always hurrying through life, seldom taking time to sit and look at something or appreciate it. He joined a little wine club that met occasionally to taste the great first-growth wines of France. He learned this was an art that one cannot hurry through. One must take time to look at the color of the wine, to hold it up to the light, to smell it, to taste it sparingly and then think about the taste. He learned of the complexity and artistry of great wine-making. This experience opened the door to a new way of relaxing, taking time, appreciating. As this particular door was opened, bit by bit his deep, beautiful spirit began to come forth and to use this relaxation and appreciation in other ways. He began to saunter on his walks instead of always hurrying. He began to linger over his conversations with his family and friends. He began to listen to music more deeply.

Finally he began to pray and meditate in depth. By now his true, deep "self" was in almost full control. To his surprise, the wine-drinking began to drop away from him, gradually at first and then more and more. He just didn't want it anymore, and his body gave him signals (he had learned to listen to the wisdom of the body) that wine was no longer good for him at this new stage of his growth. He doesn't condemn it. He still appreciates its beauty and its complexity, and he is grateful the first little door it opened for him. But he seldom drinks it. He has grown past it.

A dangerous example? Perhaps. This is not the story of an alcoholic who had allowed wine to become his master. (In such a case, radical surgery is needed by the Holy Spirit, as with all obsessions.) It is the story of a person who as he grew was prompted by the spirit and the health of the body of light to say no to something which at first had helped him grow, but now threatened to hamper his growth.

We do change. This year you may find your growing powers lead you into much activity and organization and public contact. Next year perhaps a newly released part of your spirit will draw you for a while into solitude and contemplative thought. This is not a restless kind of chopping and changing, now up, now down. It will be a steady, peaceful progress accompanied by growing power and assurance, as the spirit within is released.

And we will look back at our early activities of growing and experiences of release, not with contempt, but with a kind of amused affection. We will feel much as we do when we visit our elementary school of so long ago: "Is *that* the water fountain that was so hard to reach? Is that the auditorium that seemed so huge and lofty? And did this library really seem so endlessly full of all the books in the world? Was it so hard to learn to climb that jungle gym in the play yard?" We will see one of our teachers coming down the hall—this person who once seemed as tall as a tree and the source of all wisdom and power. Now we are of equal height, and we meet as friendly equals, even if we have gone far past our former teacher in knowledge and experience.

No, there is no disdain or contempt if we have grown with healthy balance. There may be some amusement at the awed, groping child we once were, but there will also be loving gratitude as we see the equipment, the little chairs and books, the hard-working guides and teachers who helped us grow.

And as we release ourselves to grow into new forms of power and goodness, so we can release *others*.

This is the great act of prayer and action called *"intercession."* That word is a troubling one, for it implies that we must intercede with God for others:

beg him, point out something that he overlooked, and put in a good word for the petitioner—a most degrading image. Rather we are, in our thoughts, prayers, and deeds, to *release* others into God's healing light and to the depths of their own spirits.

How is this done? In the first place, we will learn to release our loved ones, or anybody we pray for, *from our own selves*. From our possessiveness, our compulsiveness, our anxious expectations. This attitude on our part washes over into our prayers for others, so our prayer for them isn't a release at all, but a kind of brain-washing at a distance.

"How can I get my husband to be a Christian?" I am often asked, "How can I make him want to come to church? I have prayed and prayed for him, but I haven't seen any difference."

"How can I make my daughter stop smoking cigarettes?" was asked another time. "What way shall I pray for her so she won't want to smoke anymore?"

"I'm praying that my mother becomes a less quarrelsome person," said a man to me once. "She's such a perfectionist. Do you think prayer can change that?"

"My child is so restless—always jumping around and bumping into things and living at the top of his voice. How can I pray so he'll calm down?" a mother often asks.

The first thing we have to learn is that we have no right at all to pray that another person will do or be something which we have decided is right for him. We *don't know* what he'll do or be like or what he will decide when his deep spirit is released. That is solely between him and God.

63

All we may do is picture him released into God's radiant light——into God's hands, for the healing of any of his energies that may need healing. We offer ourselves up as willing channels so that God's healing energy may reach that person even more deeply, for God chooses to work through each of us for others that way. It is no business of ours how God's energy will choose to work on another person, or what will come forth from the light. *We* are not the source of his healing. Nor can we be always sure what most needs healing in that person.

If he is a compulsive smoker, for example, to be sure the smoking is a health problem, but it probably stems from a much more serious problem within. A woman once came to talk to me about her excessive smoking. As we talked, it seemed to me that she had a profound uncertainty about her own worth. She found it almost impossible to say what she felt, with confidence. The smoking perhaps was only a symptom among other symptoms. If our group merely prayed about her smoking, concentrating on that, we would not have been helping her to true release. If the *deep* problem is not solved, whatever it is, the person may merely be released from smoking to go to compulsive drinking or eating.

It is the same problem if we concentrate on someone's bad temper or endangered marriage. We don't know what deep wounds within have given rise to that bad temper or endangered that marriage.

I am *not* recommending that we psychoanalyze all our friends. I am *not* suggesting that in prayer groups we talk over and decide to our own satisfaction what a person's real problem is. We *cannot* fully know or judge these things.

But I am urging that we relinquish the *whole* person to God's light. I urge that we hold ourselves as channels for the healing of *all* that person's wounded levels, most of which we cannot either see or imagine.

I feel the same way about prayers for physical healing. Instead of focusing on the injury or sickness, I relinquish the *whole* person to the Father's healing rays, including the parts which seem to be perfectly all right.

A major point in the releasing of others is to realize we cannot hurry them into spiritual growth or freedom. Even if we know that prayer would help them, we must not nag them to begin. Even if we know that freedom is there for the taking, we can't push it on them. Some people are more afraid of freedom than they are of pain. At their present stage, they would not know what to do with freedom. We must be gentle with the growing of others, and never try to make them take more than they *can* take. *Prayer is not pushing. It is releasing and trusting.*

Love for others is not a list of rigidly prescribed deeds, nor merely a lot of friendly emotion. Deeds, though outwardly righteous, are often utterly compulsive or sternly judgmental in their underlying attitude. And feelings of warmth and emotion cannot be commanded. It is useless to exhaust our energies trying to make ourselves have certain emotions toward others. Love, like prayer, is a willingness to remain open, to receive all that one can, to give increasingly as one is released to give. Above all, love is a desire to let the other person be what he wishes to be and what he can be at that moment, without pushing him. Love is a desire for him to grow into his full spirit, but in his own way and in his own time.

As we love another person we are willing to do for him what we are learning through released prayer to do for ourselves: we accept with compassionate understanding his lesser selves (his emotional children) as they come forth to meet us. Often they will come with anger, fear, defensiveness, superficiality, flattery. We do not need either to fear and obey his emotional children or to try to exterminate them. They are part of that person, and probably need healing. But they are not his whole self or his deep self. While talking with or praying for him, we can accept his lesser selves for what they are at that moment, but at the same time speak to the deep self which underlies them—a self of mystery and beauty and power.

Let us drop the "shoulds" and the "oughts" as we relate to others. This becomes easier to do as we drop them in relation to ourselves, and trust the working of the spirit within to show us what is right or wrong for us.

If we have been hurt by a friend, slighted, ignored, belittled, let us again do the act of release. We have to deal with our own hurt feelings, of course, as we have learned to do. But let us not tie them to that person who caused the hurt. Loose him. Let him go. Hold him in prayer, but let us not hold him to our injured feelings. It is very hard to release someone from our hurt expectations if we have been truly trying to help him with all the love that is in us, and our efforts are misunderstood and resented. The reason is usually that there has been too much compulsive programming for that other person going on in our hearts, too much of a demand. It is even worse when that demand is unspoken, for it fills the air with its possessiveness, and the other person strikes out, subconsciously fighting for freedom.

We must give him freedom, even freedom to make mistakes. For only in that way will he really grow. When we pray for such a one, as we focus God's light on him, let us open the hands in our laps as a sign of letting go. Let us also open the hands of our hearts, praying:

"You are loved by God on all your levels. He surrounds your body and emotions, and your spirit, with his healing, energizing light. We release you fully to that light. Into his hands we commit you."

That is the most beautiful and the most powerful thing we can do for another human being.

# 7-Radiate

When we come forth from releasing prayer, we are not the same person who came into it. Nor is the world the same place. By the act of relaxing, realizing, reviewing, relinquishing, receiving, releasing, the atmosphere has slightly changed for everybody in this world. By this act, we have become conductors of the supreme energy of God into this dimension of time and space and to all people everywhere. Nothing will ever be quite the same as before. History will be changed because you prayed. You prayed, not with mere words, but as a living soul.

It is an awesome realization.

This fact need not weigh us down with a sense of anxious responsibility. This is the way it was meant to be, "for the creation waits with eager longing for the revealing of the sons of God" (Rom. 8:19).

The whole point of prayer is to reveal each one of us more fully as a son of God. And as we are each increasingly revealed, we help reveal that light in every other person we meet. And it is revealed, not by the traps of forced imitation, pushing the self into certain acts or feelings, but by the full, spontaneous welling forth of the light buried deep within.

That light is as deep as space, as brilliant as the sun, deathless, forever burning. For it is God's own substance.

It shines lovingly through us when our surface self does not feel loving. It pours energy into us when our conscious self is depleted. It works slowly on our physical cells, and does deep surgery on our subconscious selves. It spreads like an aura over all our relationships without a word being spoken. It touches others through us.

Other people will be keenly aware of this radiation around us and through us. Often they do not know just what it is they feel, but they will know that something they need is flowing out to them. They will sense that they are in the presence of a *living* self—life itself—not just an animated model of righteousness.

Just as a little campfire in the darkness draws wanderers to its warmth and light, so will a newly released human being unconsciously draw many to him. Some will feel threatened by this newborn power and uniqueness and beauty. They will not be comfortable, and will wish to go away.

Others will need what is offered there so badly that they will become too dependent, and draw energy and strength from the person who has become the channel of light. They do not do this on purpose. Often they do not know they are doing it. But if they have not learned to pray, have not learned to draw energy for themselves from the Cosmic Source, they will draw it from other people who have.

We must be aware of this, that it is happening now and will increasingly happen as we grow in our released light.

This is why its so important to be sure we are channeling God's energy and not merely our own conscious stores of love and goodwill. I have known many people, deeply and idealistically involved in helping others through counseling, group work, prayer, who have become so exhausted that they can hardly draw a deep breath, who hate the sound of their own voices, or the sound of the telephone ringing which announces another need at hand.

It is not necessarily because they are unfitted for their work, but because they have neglected to put themselves deliberately each day into the infinite reservoir of light, and to keep themselves there.

I made this mistake for years, including many years after I became active as a prayer leader. Some of the time I felt exhilarated and full of power. But at other times, and increasingly, I became tireder than ever before in my life. After a prayer session or an hour of counseling I would be almost trembling with cold, hunger, and fatigue. I was even ashamed to shake hands with anybody afterward, because my hand would be so icy cold. This had nothing to do with shyness or nervousness. It was a direct energy drain. Others would go away looking renewed and comforted, and I would be left, feeling like a wet washrag.

Anyone growing into a position of spiritual leadership of any kind *must* be warned about this, and learn what to do to protect his healthy balance while in the process of giving deeply.

In the first place, if you find that others are increasingly turning to you for prayer and counsel, remember that you too are a human being. Do not be ashamed that you get tired, angry, frightened, lonely sometimes. You can share the fact that you have these feelings with others, without venting your moods on them. Deal with these feelings compassionately as suggested in chapter 4. Don't pretend to anybody, including yourself, that you have grown beyond all earthly emotions and problems merely because you are becoming an active prayer group leader or member.

Second, remember that as you grow more open to your deep inner self, you will become far more spiritually, psychically, and emotionally aware of other people. You are more advanced now, but you are also more in danger unless you protect yourself.

Third, protect yourself each day and before each counseling or prayer-channeling for others by deliberately folding the light of Christ around you. It is often helpful to visualize this as if you were actually putting on a long cloak of light, pulling the hood over the head, enfolding the neck, arms, and chest. Let it fall in folds of light around the loins and legs. Draw it over the feet like shoes, and over the hands like gloves.

Some people will feel a warmth or a tingling vibration through their bodies as they do this. Others will be aware of nothing of that sort. It doesn't matter. The point is that this enfolding light is a fact. We are clothed in Christ, in the substance of eternal, divine energy, which cannot be exhausted, drained, injured, killed. This is what the Psalmist meant when he wrote:

> He who dwells in the shelter of the Most High,
>     who abides in the shadow of the Almighty,
> will say to the Lord, "My refuge and my fortress;
>     my God, in whom I trust." (Ps. 91:1-2)

You may ask, Why should we have to do this? Isn't this the same light that shines from our own deep, released spirit? Isn't this light that which attracted others to us for help in the first place? Why are we not automatically protected as we grow into release?

Yes, it is the same light of lights which shines radiantly from the depths of our spirits and which we allow to enfold us in protection. But we must take the deliberate, conscious step of protective enfoldment, because all too easily we fall back into our old emotional habit patterns. All too easily we forget to draw from the infinite reservoir of the spirit, and start drawing only from our surface emotions of love and will-power. We are apt to close the door to our true strength without even knowing we have done it. So we put the light around us deliberately, not so much to protect us against the outside world as to protect us against our own depleting emotional habits.

I find a beautiful parable of this in the Gospels, in the story of the miraculous feeding of the five thousand from the small boy's lunch bag of bread and fish. However we may interpret that story on the literal level, it is a profound statement of spiritual and psychological wisdom. As I see it, it applies to you and me in this way. Around us are hundreds of people

72

hungry for the experience of energy and growth. We who have grown somewhat are like that small boy, carrying with him some nourishment. If he had made the mistake of carrying his "five barley loaves and two fish" around to all the people *himself,* trying to feed everybody, his little lunch would quickly have disappeared, leaving most of the crowd as well as himself as hungry as before.

He was wiser than that. He put what he had in the hands of the Christ. "Jesus then took the loaves, and when he had given thanks, he distributed them to those who were seated . . . as much as they wanted. And when they had eaten their fill . . . his disciples . . . filled twelve baskets with fragments from the five barley loaves, left by those who had eaten" (John 6:11-13).

A fascinating story. Let us take it as a guide to our growing and giving in this life. We bring the little we have—our energies, our gifts, our love—first to the Christ and relinquish them to him. He will take them, bless them, accept them as channels, pour through them the infinite stream of divine, undying energy. And as we channel the feeding to others, we ourselves are also fed.

It is the Christ himself who holds open our doors to his own deep spirit and thus to our own. And we are protected against the trap of closing the door to the depths and acting again from our surface energy.

And as we rise from prayer or counseling, let us take a few minutes to place that circle of light around us again. For now we go forth to adventure in time and space, with many people and their many conflicting needs. The drain of energy will be a different kind from that of the deep counseling or the deep prayer channeling.

We go out, radiating. Because we have deliberately put the light around us, the door to our deep spirit stands open. We are now ready to accept the people and the experiences that come in his name and strength.

The telephone rings. As we go to answer it, we know that the eternal light flows out before us and will encompass the one who calls and us who answer.

We sit down to write a letter. We ask that the light and strength flow through our words and touch the one who receives it.

We go to a committee meeting. Without going obviously into prayer, we place all who are in the room and the issues at hand under this light. If one of the people present becomes upset or unpleasant, don't try to fight them on their own level. Silently focus God's light on their whole self, asking that they be helped on whatever level they need it.

We go to daily work—housework, office work, teaching, selling, whatever it is—visualizing the deathless light giving us the energy and patience we need. We hold ourselves open to new ideas and a new approach to the work. We look on it as an adventure of learning that our deep spirit is experiencing.

We drive the car. We put all parts of the car and our own driving under God's protection and light. Silently we commit other drivers we see to that same guidance. Every atom of this material universe, includ-

74

ing machines, can be touched and permeated with his light.

We go to the doctor or dentist. We relax the body, trusting God's healing power through the agency of this medical man or woman. We deliberately surround the doctor with God's light and purpose as he puts his hands on us. (Do try this. It makes an amazing difference in one's experience in a doctor's office!)

We go to church. As the minister rises to preach, as the choir rises to sing, we mentally draw this circle of white light around them, asking that God's beauty and guidance flow forth through them to the congregation. (As a minister myself, I can always tell when someone is praying for me in the congregation. The energy flow changes astoundingly!) Look around the pews nearby. If there is anyone who looks lonely, ill, depressed, bathe him in the healing light. (And don't forget to smile and speak to that person afterward!)

We find ourselves going into a temper tantrum or behind a defensive wall, or surrendering to a compulsive temptation. Take just a moment between breaths to call inwardly for help, for the swift work of the light, even if part of you doesn't want help. It will *always* come, even if only a little part of us wants help and asks for it. We never have to be in a state of 100 percent faith or willingness. Even if just 1 percent of our willingness wants help, and calls for it, that is enough for God.

We eat or talk with our family. We ask that we love them with a releasing love, not a possessive, programming one. They were God's beloved ones long before they were ours. Even at the moment of guiding and helping them, let us open the hands of the heart, and release them fully to God's light. We will then love them more, not less. And they will respond more fully, for there will be spaciousness and relaxation in our love.

We meet our friends. God's light will bathe the relationship. Let your friend be what he wishes to be. Accept and love him in his uniqueness, his difference from you, not only in his likeness to you. Be willing to go on separate paths while growing. He may, on his own path, teach you things about God you never thought of!

We read the newspaper, and our heart is sickened by what we read. Relax the body, take a few deep breaths, inconspicuously place your hand on the distressing article, and commit the situation, the people, to the radiant light of God.

We go to bed. Gently relax each part of the body, the way we have learned to do in prayer. Breathe slowly and deeply a few times. Know that the light still shines around you, protecting, releasing. It is now time for the body and the surface self to relinquish themselves trustingly to God who loves them. Now the deep self, your spirit, will continue to experience, to learn, to communicate. Visualize an open door between the sleeping body and the watchful spirit. Ask that the flow of sustaining energy be gentle and constant through the night, and that if dreams come they rise from your meaningful depths to bring you understanding. Let go deeply, for this is a time of profound renewal on all levels.

Those who have the wind of the Holy Spirit, go forward even in sleep.[1]

Radiant light goes with us, wherever we go, if we wish it. "Man became a living being," we are told in Genesis. This miracle of renewed creation can happen for each one of us today. *For that which we most need is what we most are.*

It is as *living* beings that we radiate God's light in all situations. Not as lifeless, blueprinted puppets imitating the work of his energy, going through the motions of love and righteousness.

Out of the trap! Not by our own struggles, will-power, and duty, but by the hand of the living God, reaching us through the opening door of our own deep spirit.

Released to radiate!

[1] Brother Lawrence, *Practice of the Presence of God.*

# 8-An Experience of Group Release

Can this experience of radiant release be found and shared in a group? Increasingly I am asked this question by concerned men and women who wish to help one another and to be helped toward this release of the deep spirit.

Is it really possible in a group situation? Isn't there the danger in a group that a "mystique" develops, even stronger than that in an individual, which pushes its members into a mold? Don't compulsive feelings and ritual habits develop that reinforce feelings of guilt and inadequacy? How can a group grow in strength and unity, and at the same time allow each member to grow as an individual in his own way and his own time?

These dangers exist, of course. There is always danger in any vital spiritual growth. Nevertheless, it is my firm conviction that there is no experience quite equal to that of the Christ-centered group release. In such groups, Christ not only releases the individuals at a profound level, but he also welds together these separate persons into a mighty channel of healing power.

The result is both intensification of individuality

and intensification of union. The same spiritual law operates in marriage at its best. The two have become one, but also each member is becoming more "himself" and "herself" than ever before. "This mystery is a profound one," as St. Paul says about both marriage and the union of the church with Christ (Eph. 5:32).

Let us explore this mystery of union yet uniqueness. There are several things to remember as two or more seek oneness in a Christ-centered group.

The first thing to keep in mind is the mystery of the many-faceted diamond. The light and the glory are One. The response is multifold. No group is quite like any other group. Each develops its own unique "face" as it responds to God. There is no one infallible method. A group can learn from the experiences of others, but must be willing to be led freely and flexibly into new ways.

I'm stressing this because in this chapter I will be sharing, step by step, the method and experience of a group to which I belong. The ways outlined here have been helpful for us, and may open many possibilities to others. But this is not offered as the *only* way, because it has itself been fed by the streams of many good ways.

Once I was asked to visit another group and share with them the way in which we pray and meditate together. As I went through the steps, one member said excitedly, "Lets put all this on tape and do it exactly this way at our next meeting!"

"No," said another member wisely. "We've learned a lot from this approach, and we can share this spirit.

But we must let God work these ideas into our *own* soil, and see what grows naturally there."

I applauded this healthy response. This is the true Christ-centered response to *any* kind of inspiration from any leader or group. Listen, learn, but keep your freedom of growing in your own deep, unique spirit.

A second thing to remember is whatever kind of group develops, prayer, meditation, discussion, or a combination of these, whatever methods are developed, there should be a healthy balance between concern for personal needs and concern for the needs of others. There is nothing *innately* selfish about concern for self. And there is nothing innately unselfish about concern for others. It all depends upon the underlying motive and spirit. A person freed by Christ is just as released in his receiving as with his giving. It all flows from the same source of loving energy.

Another thing to remember is that it is well to have a balance between speaking to God and listening to God, as explained in the chapter on receiving. Few groups are capable of total silence, nor would it be a desirable goal for most groups or its individual members. But groups in which there is only vocal prayer, no matter how honest and expressive, are missing a great source of growing which comes through listening deeply.

Too much silence can be threatening or boring to some members who have not yet learned what to do with silence. At first there may be much restless motion, much throat-clearing, or a stiff, embarrassed ramrod tension. It is helpful to have a little preparation. The members can share with each other the various ways they use the silence. Or the leader can read aloud a few excerpts from some guiding book, to give a little structure to the meditations. Quite soon, the silence will seem natural and be eagerly welcomed by the group, even as expert swimmers leap eagerly into the deep water.

Silence is a great and neglected power in our spiritual groups. Personally I feel that more of it would be helpful and welcome even in our large weekly church services. There can't be as much silence here as in a small group, of course, but at least there could be a couple of minutes during each Sunday morning service in which the members of the congregation (*without* soft organ music, humming choir, or murmuring minister) can look into their own hearts and learn to hear what God may be saying to them. The minister or deacon could give a few simple suggestions as to how this can be done, so no one need sit leafing through the hymnbook, or counting all the coughs!

We want to avoid extremes, even of good ways. If most members of a group are new to the concept of silence, it is best to begin with just a few minutes of it, and slowly increase the time if the group feels guided that way. Certain spiritual "muscles" are being used here, perhaps for the first time.

A major point to remember is that no pressure is to be put on any member, either to attend regularly, to pray aloud, or to have certain spiritual experiences that others are having. Concerning attendance—this is Christ's group, not ours. He is the leader, the source of energy. He will send to us and keep with us those who are right for the group. If an individual feels guided to take on this way of response to God, he will spontaneously come as often as he can. Pressure will not be needed. If he is not thus guided, or does not feel he can fully take on this experience, he will not continue to come. So what point is there in any push to "commitment," or reproachful hints or prying questions? The same holds true if the person is reluctant to pray aloud or to share his experiences. Some of our best members have sat for months in total silence in the group before they felt ready to speak aloud. And why not?

Nor should there be pressure on any member to have certain feelings or reactions which the other members think "suitable" for Christians. Whether in discussion or prayer, let each individual be where he really *is*, trusting that God will lead him past that point when he is ready. And let the other members accept where he is, without moralizing or condemning. That does not necessarily mean approval or even understanding. But we can at least give each other the gift of listening and acceptance:

Have you the right to tell another person that he must live by the standards that you have achieved through years of struggle, strife, seeking, searching? No. Give him of your hidden manna, and let the Christ appear to him in the form necessary for his unfoldment. . . .

The offering of the wine, the water, and the meat must be done gently, sparingly, permitting the other person to come in his own good time to his spiritual good.[1]

[1] Joel Goldsmith, *Leave Your Nets* (New Hyde Park, N.Y.: University Books, 1964), pp. 81, 137.

These are some general guidelines about the foundation of a released and releasing group. As to more specific matters—whether there should be a leader or whether the members should take turns in coordinating and timing the group, whether the group should always meet in the same place, how long each meeting should last—these are matters that will be worked out by each group in its own particular situation. There are many possible variations in a released group situation, and it is an exciting experience to become increasingly alert to God's strong, gentle guidance in our own special group.

Here is the experience of one of the groups of which I am a member. (Again, I emphasize that this is not the only way—but it is *our* way, which has gradually developed over several years. It is an open and flexible way, and we continue to learn, to change, to grow.)

Anywhere from ten to twenty people (men and women, of various ages and denominations) assemble in the evening at a member's home. We decided some time ago always to meet at that home, rather than move around to different homes. It is not a social gathering with refreshments, and it lasts only an hour, so it is no hardship on the host member.

Chairs are placed in a circle, and a table with one lit candle stands in the middle. This is to symbolize the radiant light of Christ which is within us and around us.

For ten or fifteen minutes after the group is assembled there is some relaxed discussion. Names are given of people who need to be prayed for. Reports are given of those already prayed for. We are careful not to slip into gossip or diagnosis. One or two of the members present may wish to share some experience, or ask for prayer for some need. It is not a stiff solemn time. There is laughter and affectionate interchange. Christ has the group in his hand, so there is no need for stiffness or anxiety or sanctimonious piety. Some member may have brought a musical record he wishes to share, and we listen to it for a few minutes. Perhaps someone wants to read aloud some especially helpful paragraph from a book, or play part of a tape. This particular group keeps conversation to a minimum, wishing to get on to the work of prayer. But other groups may wish to have a much longer time to share and talk.

Our group work of prayer falls generally into the context and flow of the seven Rs described in this book, with a few variations.

### Relax

In our group, we remind each other, or the leader reminds us, that the physical body is about to become a channel of transcendent energy. We wish to cooperate with this fully, not only to receive, but to transmit. Most of us sit erect, feet on the floor, hands relaxed and open in the lap, breathing quietly and deeply. (No big point should be made of this, however. Some members prefer, for a long time, to remain hunched over in the traditional posture of prayer. As time goes on, they usually become more consciously aware of the body's part in what the spirit is doing.)

### Realize

Leader (the words vary, but the following spirit is

84

expressed): "We are in your radiant presence, Spirit of Christ. You are burning in our midst. Your light is around us. Within us. Help us to relax. We are resting on the Father Eternal whose love has no end. We know that at this very moment your healing energy is working in us."

A short silence follows, while each member in his own way faces the *fact* of the power of God pouring through the Christ upon us. Some members may be feeling deeply emotional. Others may have mystical experiences. Probably most of us are feeling nothing special at all, one way or the other. This does not matter—what we experience or don't experience. All that matters is that *God is*. That God is *with us*. That his love at that moment *helps us* whether we feel anything or not. We waste no energy trying to summon up suitable feelings. Some may be inwardly picturing some scene or symbol of God's light and love as described in chapter 3. Others may be receptively waiting, or making a motion of the will (*not* the same as willpower) to unite with the light in deliberate choice.

### Review and Relinquish

*Leader:* "You know us better than we know ourselves. And you still love us. There are many things that trouble and block us. We don't know what to do about them. Yours is the healing. Yours is the forgiveness. It is you who give us the honesty to face these things. It is to you we relinquish them for healing, as our little hurt children within us." (Short silence.)

"That in us which is afraid or worried, we hold it in your light." (Pause.)

"That in us which is angry, we give it to you for healing.

"We hold loneliness in your light . . . grief . . . pain of any kind. . . .

"Problems that confuse us, we hold them in your light for guidance

"Anything about which we feel ashamed or guilty, we give it to you.

"We hold in your light anyone who has hurt us . . . or whom we've hurt.

"That which has given us joy and strength this week —healing of the body . . . healing of relationships . . . guidance given . . . doors opened . . . energy received . . . loving actions of friends . . . beauty . . . new challenges—we joyfully hold these in your light that they may remain beautiful and healthy in our lives.

"The subconscious depths within us that we don't see or understand, we surrender them to you, knowing that you see, understand, and heal.

"We thank you that you are teaching us to release these things into your hands. We thank you for the change already beginning in the cells of our bodies . . . the thoughts of our minds . . . our relationships. We thank you that we are becoming part of your kingdom of light."

We suggest that the leader mention these feelings and problems with a pause after each one, giving the members time to look honestly within, to see which of these "little children" are clamoring for attention, and which are so deeply afraid or repressed that they make no sound at all. This is a deeply personal work of healing that the Spirit is doing on each of us.

After this personal work on our "channelhood," we turn to the needs of others. In the chapter on release, it was suggested that prayer for others, by the individual, come near the end of the prayer time, *after* he has deeply reviewed and relinquished his needs, listened, and received. Some groups do it that way, too. The particular group of which I'm a member prefers to turn immediately to the needs of others after the personal review. These points, whether for individual or group prayer, are flexible and can be changed around according to the inner leading.

*Leader:* "Now we offer ourselves up as channels of healing, and instruments of your peace. We hold in your light these sons and daughters of yours who are needing help."

The leader reads aloud the names that have been given. (We try not to let the list get too long over the weeks, for that gets depleting. This varies, of course, with different groups.) There is a short pause after each name. During the pause, the members will be making some deliberate mental act of giving these people wholly to God—not just the specific problem, but the whole person. Some will visualize the name surrounded with light. Some may picture the Christ laying his hands on the person. Others prefer to visualize the person radiantly well and fulfilled. Some picture nothing, but hold a steady, trustful thought of God's love for each one. We do not think of this prayer as begging God to do something, or explaining something to him that he ought to know. We believe God already knows and loves each of these persons far better than we do. Delayed healing is not due to lack of God's willingness. As the sun beats down and around the little dark hut, so God tries to pour on us far more than we are able or willing to receive. Delayed healing is due to the many blocks and obstacles of our human condition, and many of these blocks are not deliberate or conscious sins at all. It may take a long time for them to be truly healed or removed. Christ's healing is not merely temporal or superficial. He heals the *whole* man, and heals him for eternity, and the work must start far below the surface. It may take a long time for outer or physical changes to show.

On the other hand, we have all seen cases in which the blocks were removed, the doors wide open, and the healing light rushed through from the deep center outward, encompassing all symptoms. This is what the world calls a "miracle." We can never tell from outward appearance whether a person is ready for such a rapid, overwhelming healing or not. So we do not presume to judge. Whether fast or slow, complete or partial, we know that healing is God's desire for us and work on us.

*Leader:* "We now hold in your light those whose names you now put into our hearts."

The group speaks aloud names of those in need who are now brought to memory. There are usually quite a few. As we grow in sensitive awareness, often the names or faces of friends will come spontaneously to mind. I look on this as a signal to pray for them.

*Leader:* "We hold in your light our pastors . . . our churches . . . our political leaders . . . those who work for peace, justice, health, especially those who are tired or discouraged . . . neglected children . . . unwanted old people . . . other purposes and people that you now put into our hearts." (Pause, for members to speak aloud any concern.) "We hold our selves ready to be used by you to reach some person, unknown to us, who is in deep pain, desperation, or darkness, and needs your light." (Short silence.)

We do not try to visualize any special person at this point. We hold ourselves in readiness to be used in the full sense, like a charged electric wire, or the vital branch of a great tree. Some members are now aware of actual physical sensations as the power of God rushes through them. Others feel nothing special. But we are sure that God is literally taking us at our word, and that somewhere in the world, somebody's darkness is being broken. Apparently it is God's will to work on people *through* people.

This work is done through us, whether we have physical or spiritual sensations or not. This cannot be stressed too strongly. As maintained all through this book, it is deeply releasing to know that God does not depend on the power of our feelings to do his mighty work. All he needs is our willingness, the inner motion of the will and purpose which says yes. The group must remind each other of this again and again, especially when some members wish to share some of their unusual experiences and sensations. They have every right, of course, to share these mystical feelings, or clairvoyant experiences, and a loving group will listen with loving interest. But let us not take these experiences as a *goal* for any group or any growing Christian. I have seen real harm done in some groups when some of the members were made to feel worried and pressured because certain charismatic experiences have not come their way. Let us rejoice for those who have them, but also rejoice that those who do not are growing in other ways, and are equally used by the Father for good. *Willingness* is the open door to God.

*Leader:* "We now hold in your light those present here tonight. We focus on each one the radiance of your love, for healing, guidance, peace, or comfort."

The leader speaks aloud the name of each person present in the room and the others mentally surround that person with the light of healing, guidance, and peace. The person thus prayed for can respond aloud in prayer if he wishes, or can receive, the gift in silence.

If any member that evening has asked for special help for relief from pain, or guidance on some problem, the leader can mention that need briefly when the name is spoken. But we believe that neither the leader nor anyone else should instruct that person through prayer on what he should be doing, feeling, or deciding. The group only holds him lovingly in the light of God. Sometimes a member of the group may go over and hold the hand of the one who has asked for special help, or put an arm around him, or put two hands on his head. This does not happen often, and when it does it is only under a deep sense of personal guidance. Or, the person might *ask* to be touched while being prayed for. There is no rule or compulsion about this.

The leader does not forget or hesitate to speak his own name aloud for prayer when he comes full around the circle. He can do it simply and without embarrassment. He needs special help that evening because he has been true minister to the group in the service of structuring and timing and coordinating.

Then the leader can say aloud slowly the names of those who cannot be there that evening, putting them in the light with loving, releasing trust (remembering not to convey any sense of reproach because they are not there). It means a lot to a member absent on business or because of illness to know that this group will definitely be surrounding him with love, light, and strength. We urge our members if they cannot be present to "tune in" on us, wherever they are at that time, and be part of the group that way. (For that matter, when anyone asks to be prayed for in the group, we can urge that person, even if he isn't a member, to join us in silent prayer at the time the group is meeting. Many people find that extraordinarily helpful.)

We also pray for other groups meeting in prayer at that time around the world, part of the vast fellowship of prayer. Our group does not hesitate to pray also for those companions who have gone through the transition of death and are unseen by us, but alive and growing and praying as part of Christ's kingdom. Neither death, space, nor time can separate those who have become part of Christ's risen light and life.

## Receive and Release

*Leader:* "We now, each one of us, wait in silence to hear what you will say, and to receive what you will give. Help us to listen. Help us to hear. Help us to receive—whatever comes, whether in words, symbols, pictures, thoughts, or a feeling of peace and strength."

This is the high point of *listening*. This is the time when we slowly learn, each in his own way, with the helpful presence of companions, to listen deeper than the demands of duty and the clamor of emotions and hear what God is truly saying to our deep spirit. This intensely personal moment is in no way selfish or withdrawn. The presence of each person enables his neighbor to become more open and receptive to the voice of God within. *In this silent listening, as the group grows in power and unity, so is the uniqueness of each person there released.* In our opinion, any prayer group totally without such a time of silent listening is a group only half helped.

### Radiate

*Leader:* "Now we fold your light around us like a cloak, for protection . . . energy . . . love for others. As we go forth on our separate ways, we go not in our own feeble strength and love, but in your light, which is endless. Even as the branch abides in the vine, so we abide deeply in you. Help us to remember and pray for one another in the week to come, and fold one another in your light. Help us to be gentle and compassionate with ourselves, relinquishing all feelings, all problems, all joys, into your hands as they arise. When we meet other people, may it be your light that streams forth from us to enfold them. Amen."

The group usually sits quietly for a few moments. We find that the sense of peace and oneness is so strong in the room that no one wishes to break at once into talk. We feel welded together as a force which far transcends anything we could have worked out by ourselves. The differences of church, theology, politics, personal taste, background, though still existing as part of our free will, are now surrounded and permeated by a joyful union.

As one member delightfully put it, "I feel as saturated with the light of God flowing through this group, as a sponge is saturated with water!" (And really, that is a good analogy. A sponge does not stop being a sponge because it is so utterly saturated with the element of water. It remains itself, but no longer a stiff, rigid, dry, and scratchy self. By uniting with water, it enters at last into its full spongehood! This rather unromantic symbol actually sums up this whole book.)

After a few peaceful moments, during which we slowly "surface," the leader asks if anyone wishes to share anything that came to him during meditation. Often symbols or inner pictures, like that of the sponge, are shared and discussed. Or somebody will speak of a breakthrough in guidance. Those who wish to maintain the stillness feel free to slip out quietly.

The group disbands with loving good wishes to one another, and promises to hold one another in God's sustaining light.

There is a wise old saying: "Whatever you are now, when you are old, you will be more so." The same thing can be said about a group's effect on us. Whatever we basically are already, a group can make us more so.

A group centered on a deep dedication is a great power. Out of groups have risen forces that imprison or destroy, as well as forces that release and create. If we are already unfree, trapped, afraid of ourselves, and seeking some power that will save us from facing our inner self, an unfree group will entrap us more deeply. No matter how noble its words or creed may be, if a group is rigidly, anxiously trying to push its members into some prescribed mold, it is not a releasing group and will not be able to help free the deep, unique spirit within each of us.

But if we choose to join or start a group that does not try to imitate or project some "mystique" or model, but delivers itself trustfully to the God who is alive— that group will be one of the strong, swift wings of our release.

This chapter is dedicated to all such groups, wherever they are, and especially to one beloved Thursday night group which for six years has helped me learn to release, and be released by others.